FEEDING THE FLOCK

RECIPES FROM THE RED PENGUIN FAMILY

JK LARKIN

Feeding The Flock

Copyright © 2021 by JK Larkin

All rights reserved

Published by Red Penguin Books

Bellerose Village, New York

Library of Congress Control Number: 2021902431

ISBN

Print 978-1-63777-022-1

Digital 978-1-63777-020-7

No part of this book may be reproduced in any form or by any electronic or mechanical means, including information storage and retrieval systems, without written permission from the author, except for the use of brief quotations in a book review.

CONTENTS

1. Paella, With Love — 1
   Stephanie Larkin
2. Basic Stuffing Recipe — 7
   David Lange
3. Cawl Mamgu — 13
   Alex Grey
4. "Do You Take Your Peppered Peppers Laying Down or Vertical?" — 23
   Diane Murray Ward
5. Dutch Apple Pie — 29
   Cecilia Vaicels
6. Easter Bread — 33
   Cecilia Vaicels
7. Gołąbki (Polish stuffed cabbage) — 37
   Melinda Hagenson
8. Hungarian Krumpli Haluska — 47
   Jim Tritten
9. Linguine With Clams — 55
   Linda Trott Dickman
10. Mussels Marinara in Oyster Bay — 63
    Elaine Donadio
11. Potlagel – Roumanian Eggplant Salad — 69
    Janet Metz Walter
12. Twice Baked Potato — 77
    R.K. Mullins
13. Zucchini Noodles with Homemade Basil Pesto — 81
    Josephine Terracina Amodeo

About the Editor — 87
Also from The Red Penguin Collection — 89

PAELLA, WITH LOVE

STEPHANIE LARKIN

SERVINGS: 6–8

∼

INGREDIENTS:

- Chopped garlic
- 1 onion and 1 pepper (or frozen peppers and onions)
- 2 boxes of vegetable broth
- 2 cans diced tomatoes
- Tofu
- Parsley
- Paprika
- Goya Adobo
- Goya Sazon
- Arborio rice
- Saffron or turmeric
- Frozen vegetables
- Lemon juice

∼

INSTRUCTIONS:

1. In a large frying pan, sauté chopped garlic (about 3 cloves) 1 large chopped onion, and 1 chopped pepper in 1/4 cup of vegetable broth. (Or you can be lazy like me and use a tablespoon of chopped garlic from a jar and a half bag of frozen peppers and onions).

. . .

2. After a few minutes add 2 cans of diced tomatoes (not crushed tomatoes - the smaller cans of diced tomatoes - like Ro-tel diced tomatoes with green chilies or something). Bring to a boil.

3. Drain a block of tofu and cut it into thin 1/2 inch slices. Add it to the pan, along with a 1/4 cup of parsley, 1/4 teaspoon of paprika, 1 tablespoon of Adobo (Goya seasoning), and an envelope of Goya Sazon, and stir for 5 minutes.

4. Add a pound of Arborio rice, 6 cups of vegetable broth, and a 1/2 teaspoon of saffron or turmeric. Bring to a boil.

5. Lower the heat to a simmer, cover, and cook for 20 minutes - stirring occasionally.

6. Add corn, peas, or other small frozen vegetables. Stir and cover for 10 minutes.

7. Stir in a 1/4 cup of lemon juice and serve.

THE STORY BEHIND THE DISH:

When I was in the 5th grade, my best friend Cristina moved to Miami from Queens, New York, where we had grown up together. Cristina's parents had escaped from Cuba as teenagers, and her family's home was always filled with beautiful works by Cuban artists as well as with the aromas of delicious Cuban food wafting from the kitchen. As we grew older—and remained close, even with thousands of miles between us—the memories of those delicious Cuban aromas never left me. When Cristina surprised me several years ago with the gift of a paella pan so that I could learn to cook that delicious food her mom had made, I knew the time had come to turn those wonderful memories of yesterday into realities of today.

While I had never thought much of myself as a cook, I looked at the paella pan as a challenge - and I was determined to rise to the occasion. With the "Lockdown of 2020," I suddenly found myself spending a lot more time in my kitchen, cooking more than I had in the last 25 years or so. Now married with a family of my own, between my own kids and their partners and their special dietary needs and preferences, my cooking became tailored to gluten-free, fat-free vegan food. Enter Paella, a terrific dish for an extended family, and easy to adapt to various dietary needs. And while I love my original paella pan, I have learned–as you can see in the photo– that an electric covered skillet works even better at cooking everything evenly and in record time. I hope that you enjoy my paella—adapted, with love, for my wonderful family—and, hopefully, for yours!

∼

Meet Stephanie Larkin

Stephanie Larkin is the "head penguin" of Red Penguin Books and Web Solutions, an independent book and web publishing company for over 15 years. Stephanie is the host of television's Technically Speaking, an award-winning educational cable TV series airing in Queens and Long Island, The Author Corner, airing on Verizon and Optimum, Between the Covers - the show for readers, and writers, and lovers of books, and her podcast Once and Future Authors, available on Spotify, Apple Podcasts and other podcasting platforms. Stephanie's goal and company motto is "Changing lives … one book at a time!"

Also by Stephanie Larkin

Write That Book!

Write YOUR Book!

365 Reasons to Celebrate!

SCORE with Social Media

Connect with Stephanie Larkin

RedPenguinBooks.com

BetweenTheCoversTV.com

RedPenguinProductions.com

BASIC STUFFING RECIPE

DAVID LANGE

Prep Time: 15 minutes
Cook Time: 40 minutes
Servings: 12 servings

∼

INGREDIENTS:

- 1½ loaves of bread
- 1 stick of butter
- 2 eggs
- 1 onion - diced
- 2 cups of turkey or chicken stock (may substitute water if cooking inside a turkey)
- ½ cup of milk
- 2 tablespoons of poultry seasoning
- 1 teaspoon salt (or to taste)
- 1 teaspoon pepper (or to taste)

∼

INSTRUCTIONS:

1. Preheat oven to 350°F.

2. In a large bowl, hand shred bread into small pieces.

3. Add in diced onions and toss with a large spoon.

. . .

4. Slowly melt one stick of butter in a saucepan.

5. Crack two eggs and whisk.

6. Add half a cup of milk to the bread and onions and mix with a spoon.

7. Add two cups of turkey stock to the bread bowl and continue to mix.

8. Pour in melted butter and eggs and mix to ensure all bread crumbs are wet.

9. Slowly add in poultry seasoning, salt, and pepper, stirring the mixture to ensure distribution throughout the stuffing.

10. Line either a cookie sheet or large cake pan with aluminum foil, leaving extra foil at the ends to fold up over the stuffing.

11. Spoon stuffing evenly across the aluminum foil-covered pan and fold foil edges up over the center to cover the stuffing.

12. Bake for 40 minutes in the oven, checking occasionally to make sure the top is browning but not getting too crusty.

THE STORY BEHIND THE DISH:

I've always loved Thanksgiving and Christmas. Besides the family togetherness and beauty of the holidays, there was always the anticipation of a delicious meal. In my family, that meant Turkey with all the fixings. There was only one "fixing" I was truly interested in—my Mom's stuffing. Mashed potatoes with gravy, green beans, rolls, cranberry sauce, and even the pumpkin pie with whipped cream could all go by the wayside so long as I had my stuffing. As a small child, I would envelop pieces of turkey in a veritable cocoon of stuffing before eating them. If I was going to get seconds, or thirds, of anything, it was always going to be stuffing. It's not surprising that when I left home, living on my own, I truly missed the delicious meals of my childhood. Store-bought stuffing never lived up to expectations. I rarely cooked a big meal as a bachelor, but I was intent upon mastering the design of a homemade stuffing, it being a critical component for bachelor holiday cheer. When I asked my mother for her recipe, she had no written directions to offer. Instead, I hastily jotted down a list of ingredients with nearly all components being measured out "to taste." This was not the scientific formula I was hoping for but it gave me enough to begin the experimentation. All I knew for sure was the taste I was trying to recreate. It's simple but effective!

Once I mastered the stuffing, my holidays came alive again. After I got married, I continued to be the stuffing chef of the family. Sometimes, my children might assist. One of my favorite photographs from my time living in England was of my young son "helping" me to make stuffing on Thanksgiving morning. As we tore up the slices of bread, together, he would occasionally pilfer a piece of bread and pop it in his mouth. The photo shows us sitting together next to a large bowl of shredded bread and, sure enough, my boy is chewing on a chunk of torn bread. Great memories!

Where did my mother acquire her stuffing recipe? From her mother? From her grandmother? In truth, she has no recollection. So, the romantic in me will attribute the design to a prehistoric ancestor. Perhaps the proof is etched upon an undiscovered cave wall in western Europe? Regardless of its origin, I can only hope that my kids may, someday, pass the recipe down to their children, perhaps adding their own twists to the recipe to make it uniquely theirs.

Meet David Lange

David Lange was born and grew up on Long Island, New York. A graduate of the United States Air Force Academy, he served for 30 years as an Active Duty officer in the United States Air Force before retiring in 2018. Colonel Lange is a decorated combat veteran, and flew numerous combat, combat support, and humanitarian relief missions during his career. He was awarded the prestigious Institute of Navigation Superior Achievement Award in recognition of his life-long accomplishments as a practicing navigator. David loves sharing stories of hope and inspiration and, in 2020, he published his memoir, "Quest: My Journey Through La Mancha."

Also by David Lange

Quest: My Journey Through La Mancha

Connect with David Lange

www.davidlangequest.com

CAWL MAMGU

ALEX GREY

SERVINGS: 6–8

~

INGREDIENTS:

- 1 Cheap cut of lamb – shoulder or neck – around 1 - 2kg weight
- 3 Sticks of celery
- 4 Big maincrop (old) potatoes e.g. Desiree, Maris Piper
- 1–2 Leeks
- 1–2 Onions
- 2kg Mixed winter vegetables e.g. carrots, parsnips, turnip, swede, celeriac
- 1 Small head of green cabbage – Pak Choi or other Chinese cabbage gives a modern twist
- 1 Bundle of mixed herbs e.g. bay, rosemary, thyme, sage, oregano (ready-prepared bouquet garni will do as well, though my grandmother would not have known that term)
- Salt and pepper to taste.

NOTE: THIS RECIPE IS VERY FLEXIBLE – DO NOT WORRY TOO much about weighing your ingredients and feel free to use whatever root vegetables you can get hold of – if you make it with love it will still be Cawl.

EQUIPMENT:

Large (around 5 – 6 litres capacity) saucepan or stockpot.

INSTRUCTIONS:

1. Put the lamb, celery, onion, and herbs into the saucepan with 4 - 5 litres of cold water (enough to cover the meat completely). Bring to the boil and simmer for an hour or so - the lamb meat should be soft and falling off the bone.

2. Remove the lamb from the stock – allow to cool then remove the bones and excess fat. Cut the rest into rough chunks.

3. Leave the onions, celery, and herbs in the stock.

4. Allow the stock to cool – skim off excess fat from the top.

5. When you're ready, bring the stock to the boil and add the chunks of lamb and the roughly chopped winter vegetables, leeks, and cabbage.

6. Allow to simmer for a couple of hours on low heat, stirring occasionally. Top up the Cawl with boiling water as needed.

7. Season to taste.

. . .

8. Serve with chunks of buttered bread and thick slices of sharp cheese – a mature cheddar is perfect.

STORAGE:

Keep refrigerated and reheat as needed – the cawl will last for around a week in the fridge. Cawl can be frozen and is a great standby comfort food.

CHEATS AND VARIATIONS:

- Leave out the lamb to make a vegetarian/vegan version.

- Give your cawl a modern twist by adding a sachet of Japanese Miso Soup concentrate for a deeper umami flavour.

∽

THE STORY BEHIND THE DISH:

Cawl (nearest English pronunciation would be *Cah-ool*) is arguably the national dish of Wales. Yet there is no national recipe – only a national argument, as no-one can agree on what exactly goes into a Cawl. Visit any family home in South Wales and they will each give you a different recipe, together with the variants and cheats that makes this the easiest thing to make. You really can't get it wrong, even though "Making a Cawl" of something means to make a complete mess of it.

Cawl is a hearty broth made from winter vegetables. People often say that it's just like Scotch Broth, Cullen Skink, or any number of hearty peasant foods from around the Celtic world. To which I say, *No!* It's Cawl, whole in itself without needing to be like anything.

Mamgu (grandmother) taught me how to make Cawl. My mother worked full-time and my father flitted in and out of our lives. I spent my early years with my grandparents–an idyllic upbringing in the beautiful countryside of rural West Wales.

Fifty years on, I often dream of my childhood home…

BRONALLT

I am walking up the lane,

flanked by dry stone walls

lovingly constructed

by my grandfather's hands.

I can peer over

into his vegetable garden.

Neat rows of peas

and beans,

humming with bees.

Further along, the compost heaps,

vast and rich as empires,

hum a different tune.

His old powder-blue Austin A40

is parked outside the stone house.

There are no windows on this side,

or any side, apart from the front,

which overlooks a small garden,

a woman's garden, with

herbs and a few flowers

for her fancy.

I open the wooden door.

The thumb-latch rattles.

It is the only door,

I am curious why there is a door in

a wall with no windows.

The door opens into the larder,

a freezer hums in the corner.

I turn right into the kitchen.

The range is as I remember,

I breathe the imagined aroma

of baking bread and

simmering cawl,

rich and savoury.

A harmonium stands

on the far wall,

a traditional hymnbook

resting open on its ivoried keyboard.

In the centre, there is an

oak table, scratched, bleached white

by scrubbing and flour, where my

grandmother kneaded dough and rolled pastry.

The rooms in the house are

defined by thin wooden panels,

though the shell is greywacke limestone,

two feet thick.

I walk into the parlour,

The fire is unlit

yet it is not cold.

I open the curtains.

My grandfather always shut them

so he could watch the tiny television

without the glare of daylight.

The furniture is varnished, dark,

a heavy dresser, ceiling-high,

made, so legend tells,

from the wood of an oak tree

felled by my great-great-grandfather.

Something about the silence

tells me that I am too late.

That my childhood here

is long gone,

and my grandparents

are no more than dreams,

dancing in the dusty

sunlight.

Nowadays, Cawl is easily made from ingredients bought at the supermarket and delivered to my door.

But my grandfather was an avid gardener, toiling through the summer to provide enough vegetables to last the whole year. A few hardy plants, like brussels sprouts, would stay in the ground all winter; others, like potatoes, would be put in store. In September, he would dry an abundance of onions before plaiting the stems into pungent strings that he would hang from the beams that crisscrossed the kitchen ceiling. In the autumn, my grandmother, who was only five feet tall, could reach up and pluck an onion from the bottom of the string. As winter advanced, she would have to stand on a chair or ask my grandfather, who was a tall man, to reach for them.

Our only source of water was the tap outside the door. Every morning, my grandmother would fill the kettles she would need for cooking and washing. There was always one kettle boiling on the stove and tea stewing in a pot. My grandfather would wash the soil from the vegetables before bringing them inside for her to cook. In a country where sheep still outnumber people three to one, lamb is abundant and cheap. No surprise, then, that it is the staple ingredient of Cawl.

My grandparents did not own a refrigerator. The range in my grandmother's kitchen was always hot, with my grandfather burning coal and seasoned wood in turn. The Cawl would sit on the side of the hotplate for a week, just warm enough to be hygienic but not hot enough to burn or boil away. Although my modern sensibilities cringe at the thought now, we never did get any tummy troubles, which is just as well given that the toilet was in a shed at the far end of the garden.

On the first day, the Cawl would be a golden liquid filled with chunky vegetables; after a few days on the range, it would thicken and darken into a rich bronze broth. Cawl is hearty enough to be a main meal; we ate it with home-made bread and local farm cheese and were grateful for our poor but plentiful life.

HIRAETH

The Welsh call it hiraeth.

That indefinable longing

for a past so sweet it

can never be equalled.

Like a cool summer

not appreciated until

the coldest winter

sweeps it away.

Like a harvest,

which seemed so poor,

until the floods of spring

stunted the next year's flowering.

Like the last slice of my grandmother's

blackberry pie; the hedgerow fruit as

aromatic as the gifts of the magi.

No blackberry pie can equal the memory,

No matter how hard I try.

There are many foods from my childhood that I've never been able to replicate. But the cawl I make today is as good as my grandmother's. I can see her hands guiding mine as I knead bread dough exactly as she taught me all those years ago.

From my family to yours – enjoy!

Meet Alex Grey

Alex Grey's poetry and short stories have been featured in a range of publications worldwide. Her sweet life revolves around narrowboating, greyhounds, singing and chocolate, yet her original view of the world has led her best friend to say of her writing 'For someone so lovely, you're very twisted!

Also by Alex Grey

Red Penguin Collections: I Can't Find My Flashlight Anthology

Connect with Alex Grey

http://idealreaderblog.wordpress.com/

"DO YOU TAKE YOUR PEPPERED PEPPERS LAYING DOWN OR VERTICAL?"

DIANE MURRAY WARD

Daiku:

"Saucy loving you. Gently spiced with bay tonight, peppering touches."

∾

INGREDIENTS:

- Extra virgin olive oil
- Minced white onions
- Fresh garlic
- Black jalapeño peppers
- Vegetarian gluten-free chorizo
- Fresh mushrooms
- Sun-dried tomatoes
- Minced scallions
- Tomato paste
- Freshly grated pepper.
- Organic Turmeric
- Bay leaf laced water for quinoa, sorghum, or brown rice boiling
- Parboil fresh peppers (unless you prefer them crisp/al dente).

∾

INSTRUCTIONS:

1. Sauté using ¼ cup extra virgin olive oil, ¼ cup minced white onions, 3 sliced fresh garlic gloves, ¼ cup sliced black jalapeño peppers, ¾ cup vegetarian gluten-free chorizo, ½ cup sliced fresh mushrooms, 3 sliced medium-sized sun-dried tomatoes, 3 roughly

minced (entire) scallions, 2 tablespoons of tomato paste, with ½ cup water.

2. Simmer adding 5- 7 twists of freshly grated black pepper, 1 tablespoon of organic ground turmeric, and rest 1 large bay leaf on top of the mixture right before covering while maintaining low heat. Taste and sauce consistency to your preference. (I prefer heft, Ahem.)

3. I flavor the filtered water used for preparing the quinoa, sorghum, or brown rice with a bay leaf and/or turmeric or ½ a low sodium vegetarian gluten-free bouillon cube while following package instructions.

4. Parboil (a total of) 3 yellow, red or green fresh bell peppers (unless you prefer them crisp/al dente).

5. Let cool and stuff your peppers either "halved or upright".

PREPARATION AND COOKING TIME:

Conduct mincing/slicing concurrently with parboiling: 5 minutes. Sorghum takes an hour, so prepare ahead of time or use leftover cooked brown rice or quinoa. Sauté for 20 minutes (tops) while determining the amounts of ingredients I use (or their omission) to your liking! Yes, that's right, I don't dictate your taste buds! You have the foundational ingredients, now run with it!

ASSEMBLY TIME:

Zero (or requiring exercises on spoon lifting and wrist acuity). Stuff peppers, then stuff your face. I use grain as the base, then place the chorizo/mushroom sauce on top. Reheat if you desire, or once peppers are stuffed, stuff your face.

∼

THE STORY BEHIND THE DISH:

I am gluten-intolerant and vegetarian. I look like I enjoy my own cooking because I do. I also enjoy cooking for my gluten giddy-and non-vegetarian family. I became vegetarian simply because I noticed that I began feeling lighter when I didn't eat meat. It was a natural progression although I always had ready access to meat, I never ate much of it by choice in the first place. I naturally filled my plate with more salad, or vegetables while a smaller portion of meat was quite satisfying. You'll note that I do not need to forfeit spice and deliciousness in my recipes. While there exists a proliferation of cookbooks of every type already on the market, "Wholesome Willing" is noticeably and deliberately different.

I've been attaching *daikus for over twenty-five years to my handmade artisan works. My work includes hand-fashioned socks, prayer beads for all denominations, and aroma-therapy jars. I was an Academy instructor and also taught in public and private elementary schools where the "International Film Forum" I developed was nurtured. I perform regularly with poets appearing on the Arts in the Basin, Nuyorican Poets Café, and Bronx Arts and Fun Hub stages. I've provided content specific book reviews on social community matters in professional publications. My work has also appeared but not limited to Presbyterian Daily, and the Bronx Memoir Project's Volume IV anthology. I am a member of the New York Public Library's Yorkville Writers and a New York Delegate and Grievance Contracts Liaison for the National Writers Union. I presently host 'The Listening Hour" courtesy of the United Moravian Church located in Harlem, New York.

Meet Diane Murray Ward

As a modern-jazz dancer and choreographer I began experimenting by infusing poetry and ASL within some works. I began emphasizing haiku, daiku (form I developed and have used for years) fiction, and non- fiction short stories and poems appearing in several venues including Presbyterian Daily, NHK Haiku Honorable Mention, and upcoming "Love Letters To Gaia" anthology of Nuyorican Cafe artists expected release this year.

DUTCH APPLE PIE

CECILIA VAICELS

INGREDIENTS:

1. STREUSEL (TOPPING):

- ¾ cup all-purpose flour
- ½ teaspoon cinnamon
- 1/3 cup moist light brown sugar, packed
- 1/3 cup firm butter (unsalted)

2. 9-inch single pasty shell:

- Oronoke Orchard frozen deep dish, or make your own

3. Filling:

- ¾ cup sugar blended together with 1 tablespoon cinnamon
- 1 tablespoon flour**
- 5 medium-size Granny Smith apples
- 2 medium-size Rome (or Gala) apples

HINT:

As cut apples are exposed to air, they turn brown. To avoid this as much as possible, spray lemon juice on the apples after cutting them. I use a small travel size spray bottle for this. It also gives a nice zing to the pie.

~

INSTRUCTIONS:

1. Adjust the rack to 5 – 6 inches above the bottom of oven. Preheat oven to 450 degrees.

2. Streusel: Blend flour, cinnamon, and sugar in a 2-quart mixing bowl. Add butter and cut in with pastry blender or 2 knives until particles are the size of peas. Chill until needed. This can be made ahead of time and stored in the refrigerator.

3. Pastry: Let frozen pie shell defrost for about 15 minutes, then put it in the oven for 10 minutes. Remove and flatten the crust and put it back into the pan. This helps avoid a soggy crust. Blend ¼ cup of the sugar/cinnamon mixture with the flour** listed under filling. Sift over the bottom of the pastry.

4. Wash apples, peel, cut in quarters, and remove the core. Cut quarters into 4 lengthwise slices. Arrange slices compactly in pastry making a mound highest in the center. Sift remaining sugar/cinnamon mixture over apples. Sprinkle evenly with Streusel, pressing it on with your hands so it stays. Place the pie on a cookie sheet. Put in the hot oven and bake for 15 minutes. Reduce heat to 350 degrees and bake for 30–35 minutes.

5. Remove to a rack to cool for 2 – 3 hours before cutting. This recipe makes 6 servings.

Cecilia Vaicels is a singer and actress. She has been baking since childhood. This Dutch Apple Pie is just one of her specialties.

EASTER BREAD

CECILIA VAICELS

INGREDIENTS:

- 7 eggs
- ½ lb. butter or margarine, melted
- 1 ½ cups sugar
- ½ teaspoon salt
- 2 packages of active yeast
- 1 Tablespoon vanilla
- 1 cup warm water
- About 7 cups of flour

INSTRUCTIONS:

1. Beat eggs, gradually add sugar. Dissolve yeast in 1 cup of warm water. Add cooled butter (or margarine), salt, vanilla, and yeast water to the egg mixture. Add flour gradually, about a cup at a time. Do not make the dough too dry. Cover and let rise overnight or about 7 hours.

2. Punch down dough. Divide in half and shape into squares or rectangles. Divide each one into thirds stretching the dough into long ropes. Braid the three ropes and join ends to make a circle. You will have two circular braided loaves. Let rise until doubled in size. Brush with beaten egg yolk. Bake in a 350-degree oven for 30 minutes.

** If you would like, you may put 2 or 3 colored, hard-boiled, Easter eggs in the braid before baking to make it look festive. Since this makes 2 loaves, our tradition has been to keep one and gift the other to another family.

Cecilia Vaicels is a singer and actress. She has been baking since childhood. This Easter Bread has been an Easter tradition that she truly looks forward to. The second loaf is shared with family, neighbors or friends each year.

GOŁĄBKI (POLISH STUFFED CABBAGE)

MELINDA HAGENSON

Total Time: About 3 hours
Servings: 18 Gołąbki

INGREDIENTS:

- 2 heads cabbage, cored
- 2 tsp. salt
- 1 large onion, chopped
- ½ tsp garlic powder OR 2 cloves fresh garlic, minced
- 2 tbsp. bacon fat (or butter)
- 1 lb. ground beef
- 1 cup cooked rice
- 1 tsp. seasoned salt (like Lawry's)
- ½ tsp. pepper
- 1 egg
- 1 28-oz can crushed tomatoes
- 3 slices raw bacon, each cut in five pieces

INSTRUCTIONS:

1. Stir the salt into a large pot of water and bring to a boil.

2. While you're waiting for the water to boil, heat a skillet and sauté the chopped onions in the bacon fat with the garlic until the onion is soft and translucent, and set aside to cool.

3. Once the water is boiling, turn off the burner and parboil the first cabbage, covered, for about 7-10 minutes, or until 8-10 leaves can be removed easily.

4. Cut 2" of the heavy vein out of each leaf to make them easier to roll. Repeat this process with the second cabbage so you have about 18 leaves set aside.

5. Spray the bottom of a deep covered roasting pan with cooking spray and cover the bottom of the pan with extra cabbage leaves (not the ones you set aside). Alternatively, you can chop the rest of the cabbage and place enough of it in the pan to cover the bottom. Set aside.

6. Combine the raw beef, cooked rice, cooled onions, egg, seasoned salt, and pepper in a large bowl and mix thoroughly but gently with your hands. Don't overwork the mixture—if you do, your filling will be tough.

7. Place a scant ¼ cup of the meat mixture in the center of a cabbage leaf.

8. Fold in the sides and roll up to make a little package. Repeat until you run out of leaves or filling.

9. Place the *gołąbki* in the roasting pan in a single layer, on top of the leaves lining it.

10. Pour the crushed tomatoes over the top and lay a piece of bacon across each *gołąbki*.

11. Cover the roasting pan and bake in a 350-degree oven for 1 ½ to 2 hours.

NOTHING THAT IS NOT THERE

by Melinda Hagenson

The *gołąbki*, whose cabbagy aroma had been permeating my kitchen for hours, had bubbled over, and wisps of smoke had begun to trickle around the edge of the oven door, but I was gazing through the kitchen window and didn't notice. My eyes sought not the palm trees and hibiscus outside, which were native to Jacksonville, Florida, but an interior image of the farmhouse kitchen at home in Jefferson City, Michigan, a thousand miles almost dead north, where I knew another pan of "little pigeons" was being assembled.

I wasn't sure what had inspired me to make *gołąbki* at home today—my Thanksgiving fare tended toward traditional American, since I spent all my other days preparing Polish food for my restaurant—but the process, and the smell, had opened a portal I'd thought had closed long ago. The odors of cabbage and onion and tomatoes didn't have this effect on me at work, but here, although it was a good smell, and pungent, it was sad. It smelled like twenty years ago.

Today, I'd made the dish myself, and it was lonely work, but before I left home, Mama, my three younger sisters, and I had formed an efficient assembly line. Rose cored and parboiled the cabbage while I made the filling and Mama the tomato sauce; then Rose peeled off the hot leaves and gave them, one by one, to Catherine, who plopped a big spoonful of the beef, onion, and rice mixture I'd made onto each one, and I rolled them up, folding the leaves just so, before passing them to our littlest sister Lizzy, who placed them, seam sides down, into one of the two big leaf-lined pans. Then Mama poured the sauce over them and lay a strip of bacon over each one before putting the pans in the oven.

Efficient. My kitchen staff still used the same basic procedure. But, here at home today, it was just me. Even my two boys were away this year, with their military Thanksgivings being hosted in Okinawa and France by Uncle Sam. This was the first Thanksgiving I'd ever spent alone, and, despite the restaurant's success, I was struggling to find much else to be thankful for.

As I stared out my window at the imagined activity in the kitchen back home, I fancied I heard dishes clinking. Murmurs of speech, the deep voices of my four brothers. Laughter. A baby crying. Whose baby? I didn't know.

This is what the family sounds like when I'm not there, I thought. Do they miss me? Do they have regrets?

I heard Papa, twenty years ago. *You will regret.*

He'd been right, but also wrong. He'd demanded I give Patryk up for adoption and never see Kurt again, and I didn't regret refusing to do either. I didn't regret either of my boys, and I didn't regret eloping with Kurt, sweet Kurt, now nearly six years dead. But I wished I'd had a traditional Polish wedding. That Mama had been there to guide me through my first weeks and months as a new mother. That Patryk and Henryk had grown up knowing their aunts and uncles, and especially Papa, who, aside from having banished me upon discovering I was pregnant at nineteen, had been a good father, a good man.

Those regrets ran deep.

I turned my face north and closed my eyes to shut out the palm trees, focusing instead on the mental image of the farmhouse kitchen. The big table, I knew, would be laden today with the buffet-style feast that in my family combined the American traditions of Thanksgiving with the Polish fare of my parents' homeland: I saw a perfectly-roasted, home-raised turkey at the center, surrounded by *placki ziemniaczane*—potato pancakes—and a casserole of sweet potatoes, topped with toasty brown baby marshmallows, rubbing shoulders with a dish of *mizeria*, the slightly sweet cucumber salad my customers craved. I envisioned a bowl of *klopsiki*—meatballs in sour cream with wild mushrooms—and a big platter of *kielbasa*—Polish sausage—and Mama's battered old gravy boat between bowls of mashed potatoes and her marvelous stuffing, which was unlike any I'd ever tasted anywhere else, with touches of ground pork and beef and hints of cinnamon and allspice.

And of course, there was a big pan of *gołąbki*. No Polish-American Thanksgiving would be complete without it.

On the sideboard, beside a traditional American pumpkin pie, I pictured *sernik*, the Polish cheesecake whose foundation was not cream cheese but homemade *twaróg*. And surely there'd be *szarlotka* —apple cake. Papa's favorite.

It didn't matter that I'd been serving these Polish dishes to my patrons at The Starling for four years; it smelled different today in the embrace of the rich aromas of the family itself, and it was that smell, the family's smell, I was perceiving. I wished in aching desperation that I could be home today, that twenty years hadn't passed since I left in disgrace, that all was well.

You will regret.

Mama and Papa might both be dead by now, for all I knew.

A fist closed around my throat, and something in me shifted as I felt my consciousness seem to crouch, like a panther. Then, with a peculiar sensation of separation, it sprang, and the riven part of me rose, leaving the physical Emma in the kitchen below me motionless, her eyes still squeezed tight. But I was no longer that woman. This oddly-separated part of me soared above her, above her house, above Jacksonville, and turned north.

There was no time to be frightened. I was in my kitchen, and then I wasn't.

The landscape rushed past below me, a golden blur like wheat in the wind. I heard only a quick whooshing sound, and there was no sense of time, only distance: the distance of a thousand miles.

The whooshing stopped, and I found myself hovering like a spirit above and a little behind a sturdy aproned woman of maybe thirty-five, with collar-length brown hair.

Catherine. She'd been only fifteen when I left home, an awkward, bookish teen.

She stood alone and motionless in our parents' dining room, her hands flat on the old oak table, facing the stained-glass dining room windows. It was the same position in which I knew my own body was still arrested at my window in Jacksonville, a thousand miles away.

I felt the rhythmic vibrations of speech, though I could hear no sound. Was she praying?

A perception of her words seeped into my consciousness, and in the sense that I was feeling rather than hearing, I understood them: *Oh, Emma, I miss you so! Happy Thanksgiving, Sister, wherever you are.*

I tried to tell her, *I'm here,* and a sudden awareness came over me that I *was* there—that some part of me that should be united with my body was now hovering in space at the farm in Michigan while my physical self, vacant, stood at my kitchen window in Florida.

A fleeting panic consumed me, and with an almost audible vacuum-like jolt, I was sucked back into myself, back into my body, back to my kitchen, my hands still flat on the counter, eyes wide open, and fully present, but disoriented and slightly dizzy.

I gripped the counter, unsure how long I'd been gone or whether I'd been gone at all.

I must have been! It was so real! I knew with certainty that Catherine was at that very moment in the dining room at the farm, thinking about me. Talking to me. Had she somehow summoned me? Had this happened because we were both thinking about each other at once? No, I thought— I wasn't thinking about her. I was thinking about everyone.

There isn't a soul I can tell about this, I thought. No soul anywhere could understand it. They'd have me committed.

The phone rang, and I answered it with hands I hadn't realized were shaking.

It was Scooter.

"I'm comin' over," he said. "Ain't no sense in both of us spendin' Thanksgivin' alone."

As I hung up, I noticed the smoke trickling from the oven and ran to rescue the little pigeons. I'd never burnt anything in my life, other than bridges.

Scooter brought beer and flowers. He's a good man, I thought. There's something to be thankful for. I remembered what I'd told Patryk five years ago— "I'm not in search of a man, and if I was, I think I could do better than this tobacco-spitting hayseed."

But I *couldn't* do better than this tobacco-spitting hayseed. He had settled for just friends, but it could have been so much more.

We sat at my kitchen table, the *gołąbki* between us, and I said Grace while my family intoned the same words in Michigan, like singing in a round.

"Smat schnago!" said Scooter, unaware, doing his best with the pronunciation. He tapped his beer can against mine with a tinny clink. "To galumpky!"

"*Smacznego*," I said, loving him for it.

Meet Melinda Hagenson

Melinda Hagenson taught college English for twenty-five years and now spends her days thinking up excuses for putting off editing her first novel, a collection of linked short stories from which "Nothing That is Not There" is excerpted. Melinda placed second overall in NYC Midnight's 2019 Flash Fiction Challenge and has received recognition for her poetry and short fiction from the Wisconsin Writer's Association. You can read her short story "A Play of Hopes and Fears" in The Independent Bookworm's anthology The Adventure of Creation.

Also by Melinda Hagenson

"A Play of Hopes and Fears." Anthologized in The Adventure of Creation. Independent Bookworm, 2013.

Connect with Melinda Hagenson

melindahagenson.com

HUNGARIAN KRUMPLI HALUSKA

JIM TRITTEN

INGREDIENTS [MAKE ANY OR ALL ORGANIC]:

- 1 pound of yellow potatoes
- 1½ cup plain flour
- 1 egg
- ½ stick butter
- 1 1/2-ounce (or smaller) tub full-fat cottage cheese (pot cheese can no longer be found in the United States)

Instructions:

1. Strain a tub of full fat cottage cheese using a fine strainer or cheesecloth. Let sit while doing the rest. Squeezing can get out a little more liquid with a cheesecloth.

2. Peel 1 pound of peeled yellow potatoes. Grate with smallest hole grater. Squeeze out liquid and transfer grated potato to a bowl (do not let the grated potato sit too long or it will turn gray).

3. Put a pot of water on the stove and bring to a boil.

4. Add 3/4 cup of plain flour to the grated potatoes.

5. Add one whole egg.

. . .

6. Add salt as needed.

7. Combine into a thick batter. Add up to 3/4 cup plain flour as needed to make the batter thicker. Add a little water if the batter gets too thick.

8. Make small dumplings. One method is to use a *spaetzel* maker. Another is to hand roll the batter into long thin shapes resembling breadsticks and then to cut them. Another method is to use a spoon and just form the dumplings (do not let the uncooked dough sit too long or the dumplings will turn gray).

9. Start cooking the dumplings right away while still making new ones. When the water is boiling, keep it boiling.

10. Poach a few dumplings and get a sense of how long they should be cooked. It will vary based on the type of pot and altitude, but we experimented with 8–10 minutes; the longer they are cooked, the softer the end product.

11. When settled on how long you want to cook them, poach the rest.

12. Set aside in a serving dish while melting the butter.

13. Pour the butter onto the poached dumplings.

. . .

14. Add cottage cheese into the buttered dumplings. Experiment with the amount and individual taste.

15. Serve right away. Does not reheat or microwave well.

THE STORY BEHIND THE DISH:

Nobody could make Hungarian *Krumpli Haluska* like my grandmother.

I've told that to dozens of people over the past decades.

Usually accompanied by describing how I ran away from home at the age of four.

With a small suitcase and a cat under my arm.

I walked down the sidewalk about five houses south on Buena Vista Avenue in Yonkers, New York to my mother's parents' house.

A working man's multi-story row house that overlooked the Palisades on the Jersey shore of the Hudson River.

Grandma greeted me with open arms.

And made me something to eat.

You see, grandma had been a professional cook in the homes of the wealthy and the powerful.

She cooked for the Police Commissioner of New York City.

She made Oysters Rockefeller for Teddy Roosevelt.

She made me Hungarian *Krumpli Haluska*.

Learned in her native village of Bodrog Szentes in the pre-World War I Kingdom of Hungary.

She also made chicken paprikash and cucumber salad with sugar.

Her roast chicken was moist, tasty, and gave off smells that enticed you into the kitchen from the moment you walked into her apartment.

She added butter and pot cheese to almost everything.

We didn't worry too much about healthy eating in those days.

So, when in 2016, I had the chance to take a tour of modern Hungary, I jumped on it.

From the moment I arrived, I asked our guides, each waiter, and finally owners of restaurants if they could make me *Krumpli Haluska*.

"Never heard of it!"

"But Grandma came from Hungary" I responded.

I tried for three weeks to find my favorite dish in every corner of the country.

Nothing.

In despair, I sent off emails and tried to reconstruct the recipe from the collective memories of our family and offered it to the chefs in the restaurants.

Nothing.

Shortly before returning home to the United States, I had the opportunity to cross the border into Szlovákia.

To the small hamlet of Bodrog Szentes, in Zemplén County.

They proudly advertise as the only Hungarian County in Szlovákia.

You see, the war (World War I) had shifted the borders and Bodrog Szentes had been given to the newly created nation of Czechoslovakia.

The village was now called Svätuše.

But it was still the same little hamlet that both my grandparents left after the war.

I had hired a guide to take my wife and me across the border to meet with never-seen cousins.

First stop was at the mayor's office.

We talked and he introduced me to his secretary who had the same last name as my maternal grandfather.

I asked both, "do you make *Krumpli Haluska* here?"

"Of course," was the answer.

We visited with relatives and ate a delightful meal.

After we were done, I asked my cousins, "do you make *Krumpli Haluska?*"

"Of course, do you like that?"

I told them of the young woman, their cousin, Julianna Fekke, who had left their village at the end of World War I and come to America where she cooked for the rich people in New York City.

They said they had considered making *Krumpli Haluska* for our meal but had decided it was too ordinary, too simple a meal, to serve to the distinguished Americans who had come to visit them.

Ah, what could have been.

Putting together what I learned on that visit, and from notes that we later found from my mother, we have reconstructed the recipe, made it twice, and now offer it to the readers of *Feeding the Flock*. Enjoy – and when you go visit Hungary, you will never find it on a menu.

Meet Jim Tritten

Jim Tritten is a retired Navy pilot who grew up in Yonkers, New York. He writes and lives in a semi-rural village in New Mexico with his Danish artist/author wife and four cats.

Also by Jim Tritten

Jim has published seven books and over three hundred chapters, short stories, essays, articles, and government technical reports.

Connect with Jim Tritten

http://www.amazon.com/James-John-Tritten/e/B001KHVMCM

http://www.goodreads.com/author/show/2487183.James_J_Tritten

https://www.facebook.com/jimtrittenauthor/

LINGUINE WITH CLAMS

LINDA TROTT DICKMAN

INGREDIENTS:

- ½ box shell noodles
- 1 large can minced clams, drained
- 6 cloves garlic, crushed
- ¼ lb. Mushrooms, peeled, thinly sliced
- 1 bunch scallions, peeled, thinly sliced
- 3 tbsp chopped chives
- ½ cup grated Parmesan cheese
- ½ cup heavy cream
- ½ cup Melted butter
- salt and pepper
- vegetable oil

∼

INSTRUCTIONS:

1. BRING 2 QUARTS OF WATER TO A BOIL.

2. Add 2 tbsp salt, 1 to 2 tbsp oil and the noodles. Cook for 10-12 minutes, or until just tender.

3. Pour cold water into the pan to stop the noodles cooking, drain and mix with melted butter and ¼ cup of cheese.

4. Meanwhile, heat about 2 tbsp oil in a large skillet. Add in scallions, mushrooms, and garlic and cook briskly for a minute or so.

• • •

5. Add clams and ¼ cup of cheese and cook another minute.

6. Add the cream, a little at a time, stirring constantly.

7. Add 1 tbsp of chives, salt and pepper.

8. Place shells in a serving dish, pour the sauce over, and sprinkle the rest of the cheese and chives on top.

Lucas, Dione. Dione Lucas' Recipes of the Month. New York: WJZ-TV, December, 1952. Print.

THE STORY BEHIND THE DISH:

It began eleven days into my life. Dione Lucas, first female graduate of the *Cordon Bleu* cooking school published her recipe for "Linguine with Clams".

It was a family favorite in our home for as long as I could remember. I think my first comment about it was at my aunt's house where I learned that it was my *mom* who introduced it into the family, *not* my gourmet chef aunt.

I had never even read the recipe until the first time I tried to make it. That's when I discovered my mother's knack for "translating" a recipe to suit. To suit her needs, the ingredients on hand, the elements she would choose to add.

For instance, nowhere in the recipe did I see:

- "add ¼ cup parmesan cheese to the serving dish before adding the shells."

- Nowhere was there a note about linguine number 18 (thin) to be used instead of the shell noodles the recipe called for.

- *Or* three cans of minced clams instead of the one that was called for.

- *OR* the extra two bunches of scallions

Mom never used six cloves of garlic, or chives. But it was her signature dish, and I learned to make it, at her side, with the recipe out, but not read. They were more like … guidelines. It became a Christmas Eve staple, along with shrimp cocktail in lieu of the traditional "Feast of the Seven Fishes."

Once, as the fire department was putting out a fire in our house, Mom kept cooking linguine and clam sauce … so it wouldn't burn and because after the fire she knew we'd be hungry. Thank God we did not have to evacuate the house.

As she neared the end of her life, she would come to my house to have it and say, "Gee, you're the only one who knows how to make that right!" The supreme compliment.

It remained my own family's Christmas Eve centerpiece, no matter what else was served or where we were. We had it in on the island of Kauai, we had it in Redding, England, we made it in the wiles of Maine at a rented house near a nursing home where my mother-in-law convalesced.

Now the girls are grown, living on opposite sides of the country.

I got the phone call, "Mom, may I please have the recipe for Linguine with Clam Sauce?" Sure. So I sent Dione's signature recipe.

New phone call, "Mom, this is not the way you make it!"

My future son-in-law called for the recipe, so he could ignore it and make it his own.

Linguine and Clams, the 'Next Generation'? Make it so!

Dear Dione, culinary maverick, what did you start?

>Colander Girls
>
>*Carefree AZ*
>
>Old and aluminum,
>
>propped up on a trinity of curls,
>
>punched through with heart patterns
>
>that will never know your touch again.
>
>The strands of #18
>
>thrown in just to check, taste for *al dente*
>
>Then continue boiling for two more minutes.
>
>Always, two more minutes.
>
>I ladle in a little sauce, a little parmesan
>
>Strain the finally finished pasta
>
>A little more sauce, a little more cheese
>
>Served in a pasta dish made in Italy.
>
>Served on your sea blue plates *da casa*.

The water boils, I see young Teresa

learning to form pasta: flour

to form a hollow volcano

filled with the runny sun.

Worked by hand

sliced, dried out on the back porch.

The steam rises from the draining pasta,

I see Josephine who looked on,

but was never taught.

Joanie who soaked it all up

always added something extra.

Improved it with every attempt

until finally, she *was* the standard.

I add the sauce to the dish,

Steam rises once more.

The aroma, *stupefacente*.

Theresa who calls for the linguine

With clam sauce recipe, my signature,

she wants to serve it in Seattle.

Joanna who gives the recipe to Dave,

so he can adlib in Babylon.

All these things, as the water drips

through the heart shaped holes.

Meet Linda Trott Dickman

Linda Trott Dickman has been writing poetry since her first sleep-away camp experience when she was ten years old. She is a recently retired school librarian. Linda is the author of Robes: The Art of Being Covered, The Air That I Breathe and Road Trip. Linda's poetry has been published on-line, in several anthologies, an international journal. She is the current coordinator of poetry for the Northport Arts Coalition (Northport, NY.) Linda has been teaching poetry to children for over 35 years and co-leads a poetry workshop for adults at Samantha's Li'l Bit O' Heaven coffee house in East Northport, NY.

Also by Linda Trott Dickman

Robes

The Air That I Breathe

Road Trip

Connect with Linda Trott Dickman

Facebook - Linda Trott Dickman

Blog - https://libearyn.wordpress.com/

MUSSELS MARINARA IN OYSTER BAY

ELAINE DONADIO

INGREDIENTS:

- 2-3 lbs. mussels
- 1-2 (28oz.) cans crushed tomatoes
- 2-3 cloves fresh garlic, peeled
- Salt, pepper, dried or fresh parsley to taste
- Optional: oregano, hot red pepper flakes
- Optional: juice of ½ lemon (for tang)
- Optional: ¼ cup red wine (for zing)

INSTRUCTIONS:

1. Use a deep skillet or pasta pot. Decide if you will serve over pasta or with crusty Italian bread and adjust amounts of tomatoes and seasonings accordingly. Place cleaned mussels in a pot, pour canned tomatoes on top, add all other ingredients. Cover, bring to a low boil on medium heat. Simmer for 15 minutes, covered, until all shells are opened. Stir from bottom once or twice during cooking with a wooden spoon to blend ingredients.

2. Discard any closed shells immediately. Serve over your favorite pasta—recommendations: spaghetti, thin spaghetti, capellini, bucatini, linguine—or with crusty Italian bread for dunking. That's what Italian sauces are for! Serve with a side salad for a complete meal or alone as a hearty appetizer.

By the way, most Italians do not put grated cheese on any seafood dishes. Of course, the choice is yours.

The Story Behind The Dish:

One of my fondest family memories is boating in and around Oyster Bay, a charming seaside town on the North Shore of Long Island, New York. My husband, two young children, and I would drop anchor and spend the night on our boat. We spent many a weekend lazing around, swimming, wading to the sandy beach, and collecting seashells. In the evenings, we would tie-up at the dock of a nearby harbor restaurant and enjoy local seafood, socializing with other boaters and restaurant patrons.

Awaking at sunrise one lucky day, the low tide revealed a trove of undiscovered mussel colonies attached to rocks some twenty-five feet away. My stirrings roused my four-year-old son, while my baby daughter and husband were still asleep. Always ready with my versatile pasta pot, my son and I jumped off the boat and headed to our adventure.

As we began to remove the mussels from their beds, we quickly realized that this work was too dangerous for little hands. The jagged shells, rocks, and barnacles of the habitat were intent upon leaving bloody scratches on our hands. My son was relieved to have the job of holding the pot steady on a large, flat rock, while I forged on. When the pot was filled to the brim, we proudly returned to our boat with our bounty in hand. Luckily, the Harbor Master was within shouting distance and assured me the mussels were safe to eat. "If you can't fit them in your refrigerator and don't have enough ice to keep them cold, eat them now."

. . .

What a great idea! Mussels for breakfast. Why not? We moved the boat to the dock where I used the hose to rinse all the sand and debris, leaving a few inches of clean cooking water in the pot. We returned to our spot, dropped anchor, and started the cooking process. Since I wasn't prepared with any seasonings, we ate those mussels plain. I couldn't believe how delicious they were.

The next weekend, I came prepared with a few sure-fire ingredients I knew would make a tasty dish with a minimum of fuss. My Italian mother taught me well and since I had already been cooking this dish for a number of years, I knew just what to do.

If you decide to harvest from your favorite mussel colony, please be sure to check online by Googling *shellfish regulations* or *calling local authorities* to verify that the waters are not polluted. Harvest only large, closed mussels with unbroken shells. Separate the mussels from their beds with a twisting motion. It's a good idea to wear thick rubber gloves to protect your hands from cuts from the sharp protrusions. Store in a refrigerator or on ice in a bucket with seawater, or topped with wet paper towels or bunches of seaweed. Keep them cold until ready to eat. Remove the fibrous beards with a yanking, twisting action. Rinse off the sand and debris by filling the cooking pot with fresh, cold water, and dumping the water with the pot lid slightly ajar to allow the water to run out. Rinse at least three times or until the water runs clear.

. . .

Good news! You can also buy cultured mussels from your favorite seafood supplier, but it's still a good idea to rinse them well in cold water before cooking.

Enjoy!

~

Meet Elaine Donadio

Author. Poet. Blogger. Book reviewer. Reading Specialist at New York City Schools, Elaine Donadio's characters reflect the urban lifestyle. She writes about what she loves, using well-researched facts to feed your head, your heart, and your soul. She's concerned about the effects of human carelessness on the world in which we live. Learning is the point but better viewed through experiences that communicate awe as the world unfolds its secrets. Readers can laugh and learn at the same time.

Study guides in alignment with state standards for science, social studies, and literacy are available at <u>elainedonadio.com</u>.

Also by Elaine Donadio

The Montgomery School Kids Series

The Science Project

The Ocean's Way

Who Do Voodoo?

March of the Blue Moon

Other Books

The Ocean's Way Poetry Companion

Sojourn Into The Night—A Memoir of the Peruvian Rainforest

Short Stories and Poems

"Shape Shifters of the Shinulaktup" Red Penguin Books (2020) *Anthology: I Can't Find My Flashlight*

"New Orleans" Red Penguin Books (2020) Anthology: *The Beauty Within— Stories of Spirituality, Faith and Love*

"New Orleans" Red Penguin Books (2020) Anthology: *Stand Out!*

Connect with Elaine Donadio

https://elainedonadiowrites.wordpress.com/

www.facebook.com/ElaineWritesNow

twitter.com/ElaineDonadio1

www.linkedin.com/in/ElaineDonadio

POTLAGEL – ROUMANIAN EGGPLANT SALAD

JANET METZ WALTER

Servings: 4

INGREDIENTS:

- 1 large eggplant
- 1 or 2 hard-boiled eggs (depending on the size of the eggplant), chopped
- 1 medium tomato, chopped
- 1/2 small onion chopped or 1 large scallion, chopped
- 2 Tbs oil
- 1 Tbs white vinegar
- ½ tsp sugar

∼

INSTRUCTIONS:

1. Wash eggplant, poke holes in it with a fork, and either microwave on high for about 6 minutes on each side or bake at 350° for about 30 minutes until it collapses and can be pierced easily. Add cooking time if necessary–it should feel soft to the touch.

2. Let cool until you can handle it. Slit down the center lengthwise with a sharp knife. The insides should be soft. Remove as many seeds as you can with a spoon and scoop eggplant from the skin. Put the eggplant in a food processor. (If you are old fashioned and still have a wooden chopping bowl and chopper, you can chop the eggplant by hand.) Process or chop lightly until it is roughly the consistency of mashed potatoes.

. . .

3. Add remaining ingredients and stir together. Add more oil and vinegar to taste.

NOTES ON THE EGGPLANT PREPARATION:

Choose a firm eggplant that does not feel too heavy. The heavier the eggplant is, the more seeds it contains. The seeds are tiny, and although most people probably chop the seeds right into the salad, I prefer to remove them once the eggplant is cooked.

When you slice an eggplant crossways and use the slices to make eggplant parmesan, for example, you cannot remove the seeds and they are hardly noticeable. When you bake the eggplant for Potlagel and slice it the long way after baking, the seeds show up as long clusters that can be easily removed.

Since the cooking process is only to soften the eggplant and, to me, does not affect the taste of the finished product, I prefer to microwave it. There is no set time. It depends on the size of the eggplant, but 15 minutes at a medium setting usually does the trick. You need to turn it over in the microwave halfway through. The eggplant needs to be very soft. It collapses as it cooks so you can tell when it is done. You can't really overcook it, but you can undercook it. You can also bake it in the oven on a cookie sheet at 350°, but it can take upwards of 30-45 minutes. The most important thing to remember is to poke the eggplant with a fork in several different places before you cook it or the steam will build up inside and you will have quite a mess to clean up.

Sometimes eggplants tend to be bitter, hence the small amount of sugar in the recipe.

THE STORY BEHIND THE DISH:

Yes, it is spelled correctly! When my great grandparents came to America in 1887, fleeing from persecution and pogroms against Jews, they came from Roumania. The name was changed to Romania in 1975 for various political reasons.

Although I always thought I was of Eastern European descent, I found out from Ancestry that I was partially of Mediterranean descent. This puzzled me until I did some research and found out that Roumania, according to Ancestry, is classified at least partially as Mediterranean. There is some controversy as to whether it is the Mediterranean, Balkan, or part of Eastern Europe. This is probably because of wars, land acquisitions, border changes, and political alliances.

The Jewish population of Roumania was a combination of Eastern European, or Ashkenazi Jews, and Sephardic or Mediterranean Jews. Now, Romania partially identifies with the Mediterranean culture in language, religion, and architecture. When it comes to cuisine, however, it seems that the Mediterranean influence has been even stronger.

My grandfather was a year old when he arrived here. He had eight other siblings who were all born here. His mother was a good cook and cooked many of her Roumanian dishes for her family.

My grandmother, on the other hand, whose family came from Russia, was born here. She was not much of a cook, surprising for those days, but times were changing. My grandparents only had two children, and my uncle was a very picky eater, so my grandmother kept it simple.

My mother, it turned out, liked to cook and learned how from her Russian and Roumanian grandmothers.

POTLAGEL – ROUMANIAN EGGPLANT SALAD

. . .

Potlagel is one of the most famous Roumanian dishes, but very few people in my life called it by its correct name; everyone called it "Grandma's Eggplant Salad", making it the most popular dish that no one knew the name of. The closest dish that one might be more familiar with is Greek Babaganoush, which is smoother and creamier.

I recently read that there are 2500 varieties of apples grown in the United States. That is about how many variations of Roumanian Potlagel there are. They vary from just the seasoned baked chopped eggplant, to spread on bread, to variations with a variety of vegetables added to the salad.

The most common addition is red pepper. That may have been my great grandmother's original recipe. Our family, however, were not great lovers of peppers and it is possible that my mother substituted tomatoes instead. I have seen photos of Potlagel garnished with tomatoes so I really am not sure. What I am sure of is that it became a staple at every family function, and I have passed down the recipe to other family members as well as contributed it to recipe books from various organizations.

Keeping my family tradition alive, I prepare the salad in a coated wooden bowl and chop it with an old fashioned hand chopper that I have owned since I was married, many years ago. This was the way my mother prepared it. You can use a food processor as long as you don't over-process it and keep some texture to it. Feel free to modify it in any way you choose. Add something, leave something out but just enjoy your own creation.

Meet Janet Metz Walter

Janet Metz Walter grew up in Queens New York. She realized very early in life that she wanted to write, at the very least as an avocation.

Throughout her career in various Social Service agencies, she was involved in writing local newsletters and professional articles, as well as writing and producing shows in camps and local community productions.

She also has been a travel agent, world traveler, and Mah Jongg teacher.

Since her degree is a BS in Home Economics, she of course had to contribute a recipe to "Feeding The Flock.."

Several years ago she joined her husband in his e-commerce jewelry business Gold Fire Diamonds, which led to the idea and creation of "The 2 Carrot Ring and Other Fascinating Jewelry Stories," finally realizing her lifelong dream.

Since writing the book Janet also contributed a memoir, "I Really Can Sing" to the book "Realiteen: Reflections on Growing Up," part of the new Red Penguin anthology series, and hopes to continue writing.

As people hear about and read "The 2 Carrot Ring..." they have been telling her their own jewelry stories, in hopes that they will be included in a sequel someday.

Also by Janet Metz Walter

The 2 Carrot Ring and Other Fascinating Jewelry Stories

Connect with Janet Metz Walter

Facebook - Janet (Metz) Walter

Amazon.com/author/janetmetzwalter

Goodreads author Janet Metz Walter

www.goldfirediamonds.com

TWICE BAKED POTATO

R.K. MULLINS

INGREDIENTS:

1. 4 large baking potato
2. 3 tbsp Sour Cream
3. ¼ tsp Salt
4. ¼ tsp Pepper
5. 1 can tiny shrimp
6. 1 can lump crab meat
7. 4 strips of bacon
8. ½ cup shredded cheddar cheese
9. 2 tbsp chives
10. ½ tsp Cajun seasoning
11. ¼ cup Sea Salt

∼

INSTRUCTIONS:

1. Preheat oven to 350 degrees. Wash potatoes and coat with sea-salt. Place potatoes on cookie sheet and bake for 1 hour or until completely soft. Remove and let cool.

2. Place bacon in frying pan and fry until crispy. In a large bowl, cut the top off the potatoes and set aside for later. Scoop out the soft potatoes into the bowl. Add the sour cream, salt, pepper, cajun seasoning, chives, shrimp, crab meat, and cheddar cheese. Be sure to leave enough cheese to sprinkle on top. Crumble up the bacon and add it to the bowl. Mix well.

. . .

3. Scoop the filling back into each potato, sprinkle cheese on top, and replace the cut tops of the potatoes. Place back into a 350-degree oven and bake for 30 minutes. Let stand for 5 minutes and serve.

THE STORY BEHIND THE RECIPE:

I made this recipe one summer day when I was looking for something new to fix for me and the family. I had no clue what to make when one of my kids said a baked potato would be nice. I wanted something with seafood, so I thought, why not combine seafood and potatoes? Everyone loved them and started asking me to fix them more often. That was some 20 years ago. I have been making this dish ever since. If you like, you can add uncooked lobster to the filling mix or any other seafood desired. I have substituted cheddar cheese with other cheeses, like Gouda, or any smokey cheese. If you like it spicy, add more cajun seasoning. I have cut it back some for this recipe because there are those who can't eat spicy foods (for the life of me I don't know why). I really hope you enjoy this recipe as much as my family has over the years.

Meet R.K. Mullins

Growing up in the small town of Big Stone Gap, VA. I sent a lot of time down on my grandparents farm. When I wasn't working on the farm, I was always hanging out in the kitchen.

I learned to cook from my mother and grandmother. Both excellent cooks in their own rights.

Later I moved to Baton Rouge, LA. and adapted Cajun Cuisine into my cooking skills. I was never one to just follow a recipe. I had to push the limits and make it mine.

Also by R.K. Mullins

Time for a serial Killer: A Lifetime of Murder

Coming soon:

The Drunken Savior

Confessions Before Death; Satan's Revenge

Connect with R.K. Mullins

https://www.facebook.com/ronald.mullins.75

ZUCCHINI NOODLES WITH HOMEMADE BASIL PESTO

JOSEPHINE TERRACINA AMODEO

Servings: 2, but can be doubled

INGREDIENTS:

1. For Zoodles:

    - 4 whole medium-sized zucchini (peeled or unpeeled)
    - 2 chopped garlic cloves
    - 1 tsp olive oil
    - Mandoline or Spiralizer or by hand with a vegetable peeler to make the zoodles

2. For Pesto:

    - 1 tsp of pistachio nuts
    - ¼ cup of olive oil
    - 1 cup fresh basil leaves
    - 2 garlic cloves
    - Salt and pepper to taste

3. Toppings:

    - Dash of cayenne pepper
    - Dash of chili pepper seeds
    - Dash of grated Pecorino Romano cheese
    - Crumbled cashew nuts (optional)

INSTRUCTIONS:

1. For Pesto Sauce: Put all ingredients except the oil into your food processor and pulse until the leaves and garlic are chopped.

. . .

2. Pulse again and pour in the olive oil as the processor is running until a creamy consistency is reached.

3. Taste the pesto and add salt and pepper to taste.

4. For Zoodles: After making the zoodles, pour the olive oil and chopped garlic into a sauté pan.

5. Heat the oil and garlic on low and slowly add the zoodles.

6. Sauté for about 2 minutes, stirring often until tender. Don't overcook.

7. Add salt and pepper to taste.

8. Sprinkle on cayenne pepper, chile pepper seeds, crumbled cashew nuts, and a dash of grated Pecorino Romano cheese.

THE STORY BEHIND THE DISH:

Growing up as a first-generation Italian, my mother Maria always grew organic vegetables in her garden that she used in her daily cooking. Every meal was authentic and never excluded fresh, leafy greens.

My mother's Sicilian roots carried a strong presence in her kitchen and I, like her budding sous-chef, carried her traditions to my own kitchen today. Many of the recipes she created carried one simple, yet powerful ingredient–the mother of all green leaves often referred to as *the great,* commonly known as basil. My mother grew basil in abundance. Tomato and cucumber salads were a staple meal and she topped them with fresh chopped basil, of course. Tomato sauce canning included a basil leaf or two in the hundreds of jars that we canned every summer.

The one recipe that stood out, however, and will always remind me of her and of home is fresh basil pesto. I still remember picking the leaves, washing them, and laying them all out to dry. My mother used the classic pesto sauce recipe that originated in Genoa, Italy. Basil, garlic, olive oil, grated pecorino cheese, and pine nuts. Making pesto sauce was like canning tomato sauce. It was made to last. We used what we made for that night's *pasta e' pesto* dinner, but the rest were packed into small servings and frozen for many dinners to come.

It was my absolute favorite dish as a child and ironically, it's my oldest daughter Giuliana's favorite meal today. In fact, she is such a pesto connoisseur that she compares every pesto dish she tries to my mother's.

Many pesto variations have been created over the years, but the recipe I share with you today is a variation of my mother's with a healthy and modern-day twist.

Enjoy!

Meet Josephine Terracina Amodeo

Josephine Terracina Amodeo, teacher at a top ranked Long Island school district, currently a stay-at-home mom to three beautiful children, loves perfecting new recipes. She is the the co-contributor of @hummusandbasil on Instagram where many of her recipes are shared. Growing up, she spent her summers in Cefalu, Sicily, her father's birthplace, at her grandparent's home. She often tries to recreate the authentic meals her mother and nonna made as well as those memorable dishes she tried at the local restaurants. Over the years, Josephine has become a foodie and is passionate about making traditional Italian meals with a modern twist. At her new home in Connecticut, Josephine's preferred date nights are cooking with her husband who often compliments the meal with a finishing touch. You often find Josephine at the farmer's market sourcing new and exciting ingredients that inspire the next dinner. She enjoys exploring new restaurants with her family and attending featured local food events with her friends.

Connect with Josephine Terracina Amodeo

https://www.instagram.com/hummusandbasil/

ABOUT THE EDITOR

JK Larkin is a Long Island based writer and recent graduate of Marymount Manhattan College. On top of his position as Literary Manager and Editor of *The Red Penguin Collection*, JK works at The Mary Louis Academy as the coach of their Speech & Debate Team, coaching students to perform excerpts of dramatic literature, prose, and poetry for weekly competitions on both the local and national levels. His body of work draws heavily upon themes of existentialism, morality, and the struggle to connect in a deeply divided world. This past year, JK published his first two collections, ***not kidding.*** and ***Side Street***. Follow him at @jksnotkidding on Instagram or @JKLarkinTM on Facebook to keep up to date with his artistic journey.

ALSO FROM THE RED PENGUIN COLLECTION

Realiteen: Reflections On Growing Up

What Lies Beyond: Sci-Fi Stories of the Future

A Trip For The Books

I Can't Find My Flashlight

The Moments

The Beauty Within—Stories of Spirituality, Faith and Love

'Tis The Season—Poems to Lift Your Holiday Spirits

We Made It!—Essays Reflecting On The New Year

Stand Out—The Best of the Red Penguin Collection, Vol. 1

It's The End Of The World As We Know It

A Heart Full of Love—A Collection of Romantic Short Stories

www.ingramcontent.com/pod-product-compliance
Lightning Source LLC
Chambersburg PA
CBHW071024080526
44587CB00015B/2480